Meet the author

Although she can't actually swim, Lisa Hughes is an expert surfer who has written extensively about the Internet for many magazines. Proud to call herself a Nethead, she couldn't live without email and spends more time sending messages to her friends than she does seeing them. Her other interests are reading detective stories, gardening and watching football, so it's not surprising that her favourite Web sites are MysteryNet, Gardening.com and the Arsenal Football Club Home Page.

Acknowledgements

All screen shots in this book appear courtesy of the producers of the Web sites they depict and remain the copyright of those producers. Every effort has been made to contact the copyright holders of the screen shots in this book. If any rights have been omitted the publishers apologise and will rectify this in any subsequent editions.

Examples of ASCII art by Win Kang and Mike Rosulek from Dave's ASCII Art Page at http://nunic.nu.edu/~dissel/dave.txt

All trademarks are acknowledged.
Apple, the Apple logo, Macintosh, QuickTime and any other Apple products referenced herein are trademarks of Apple Computer, Inc, registered in the US and other countries.
Eudora is a registered trademark of the University of Illinois Board of Trustees, licensed to Qualcomm Incorporated.
Java and the Coffee Cup are registered trademarks of Sun Microsystems, Inc in the US and other countries.
Microsoft, Microsoft Internet Explorer, MSN, and any other Microsoft products referenced herein are registered trademarks of Microsoft Corporation in the US and other countries.
Netscape Communications Corporation has not authorised, sponsored, endorsed or approved this publication and is not responsible for its content. Netscape and the Netscape Communications corporate logos are trademarks of Netscape Communications Corporation.
Worlds is the registered trademark of Worlds Inc.

Introduction

Lots of things that you can do in the real world, you can do on the Internet. That includes having fun because the Net is one enormous playground. What's also great about the Net is that once you're online you become part of a community – and it's a very big community, too.

On the Internet you can meet people, you can travel far and wide, you can see weird and wonderful things. You can keep in touch with your friends, follow up a hobby or find information to help with your homework. This book will show you how to do all these things – but you'll have to do a bit of reading first because, like anything to do with computers, you need to learn some technical stuff before you can get started.

All the information in this book was checked carefully before it was published but the world of the Internet changes so fast that you may find some of the details are out-of-date and the Web sites we talk about have changed – or aren't there any more. However, if this is the case you can be certain that something even better has taken their place, so use your skill and imagination to find it!

This book will help you launch yourself into cyberspace, so what are you waiting for? Fasten your seatbelt, get set for lift-off and have a brilliant time!

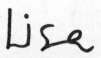

The Internet

Lisa Hughes

Illustrated by Tim Benton
Consultant: Bill Thompson

Hodder
Children's
Books

a division of Hodder Headline plc

This book is for Jeanne, Mike and Rich – none of them Netheads but all supportive in their different ways – and particularly Tamsin, for the good times we've had wandering the Web together. I get my technical support from Angus and my Internet access from Easynet – both are very reliable and I'd like to thank them both very, very much.

Text copyright 1998 © Lisa Hughes
Illustrations copyright 1998 © Tim Benton
Published by Hodder Children's Books 1998

Series design by Fiona Webb. Book design by Mei Lim

The right of Lisa Hughes and Tim Benton to be identified as the author and illustrator of the work has been asserted by them in accordance with the Copyright, Designs and Patents Act 1988.

10 9 8 7 6 5 4 3 2 1

ISBN: 0 340 71514 – 6

A catalogue record for this book is available from the British Library.

The information in this book has been thoroughly researched and checked for accuracy, and safety advice is given where appropriate. Neither author nor the publishers can accept any responsibility for any loss, injury or damage incurred as a result of using this book. The publishers cannot be held responsible for any of the material which may appear on the Web sites listed in this book.

Hodder Children's Books
a division of Hodder Headline plc
338 Euston Road, London NW1 3BH

Contents

What is the Internet?

What the Internet is • How it works
• Where to access it

You've probably heard a lot about the Internet, but what is it?

The Internet is a computer network that uses the telephone system to link together millions of computers around the world. Maybe that doesn't sound incredibly exciting but once you're connected to the Internet, there are lots and lots of different things you can do. You can send electronic messages or 'email' to your friends (as long as they're on the Internet too), or you can sort through all sorts of information on something called the World Wide Web.

You don't need to know how the Internet works in order to use it, but if you understand the basics it may help you solve any technical problems you have – and of course you can impress your friends with your Net knowledge!

How does it work?

You may think that your telephone is just for talking. But as long as you have the right equipment, you can use a telephone line to transmit computer data as well as sounds. If you plug your computer into the telephone system it can receive information from, and send information to, other computers (as long as they are plugged into the telephone system too).

Transmitting computer data

Computer data is made up of electronic signals. A computer language called TCP/IP (which stands for Transmission Control Protocol/Internet Protocol if you like to know these things) is used to move computer data around the Internet.

Many of the links in the Internet, for example those which transmit computer data across the Atlantic Ocean, are special, fibre optic cables. Fibre optic cables use light to transmit information. They can carry a lot more data than an ordinary telephone line and they send it a lot faster!

There are all sorts of computers connected to the Internet. Most are small machines sitting on people's desks but many are powerful computers in universities, government offices or large companies.

The individual computers and cables which make up the Internet are owned by people and organisations, but no one actually owns the Internet itself. This means that no single company or group can control what happens on the Internet – so anything can happen!

How big is the Internet?

Because no single organisation runs the Internet, no one really knows how many people are connected to it. It's thought that there could be 60 million people on the Net, connected up to over 15 million computers! Join up and you could be number 60,000,001!

How can I get on the Internet?

There are lots of places where you can access the Internet. Your school may have an Internet connection which you can use during lessons or free time. Libraries often have computers connected to the Internet for members of the public to use.

Or you could go down to your local cybercafé. Most cities and large towns have at least one cybercafé. Like ordinary cafés they sell drinks and snacks, but they have computers too. Cybercafés charge people to access the Net but it doesn't usually cost very much to use it for half an hour. Make sure you don't get crumbs in the keyboard, though!

If you're lucky, you may already have an Internet connection at home. If you haven't, see if you can persuade someone to get one for you!

2 Getting connected

Hardware • Modems • Internet access providers • Online service providers • What it all costs • Internet software

The Internet involves all sorts of technical stuff so unfortunately it's not one of those things you can just sit down and use. Learning the basics isn't difficult but in the early stages you may need to be quite patient. Stay with it, though, because it's definitely worth the effort.

If you're going to use an Internet connection that has already been set up, you can skip ahead to chapters 3 and 4, because they explain how to use Internet software.

If you're going to set up your own Internet connection at home, you need to read this chapter. You might also want to show this part to any adults who might be around so that they understand what to do, too.

What hardware (equipment) do I need?

To access the Net you need a computer. Most computers bought in the last three years can connect to the Net, but you may need to upgrade older machines.

To access the Internet efficiently, IBM-compatible PCs should have a 486MHz or faster processor, at least 8Mb of RAM and around 500Mb of free hard disk space. You also need a colour screen, a sound card and a video card. With Apple machines, the processor should be at least a 68030 with 8Mb of RAM and 500Mb hard disk space.

If you don't understand this 'specification', don't worry. Ask someone to have a look and tell you whether your computer matches up to it. If your machine has a lower specification, it may still be possible to access the Internet but check with someone who knows about computers.

A small but vital box

As well as a computer, you'll need a box called a modem which sits between your machine and the telephone system. One cable from the modem plugs into your computer. Another plugs into the phone socket. A modem is a vital bit of kit. This is because all computer data is digital but it needs to be in a format called analogue to travel down telephone lines and across the Internet. The modem translates data from digital to analogue – and back.

Modems send and receive computer data at different speeds, measured in Kilobits per second or Kbps. Your modem should be capable of speeds of at least 14.4Kbps or, preferably, 28.8Kbps. Otherwise, using the Internet will be quite slow. Modems with speeds of 33.6Kbps or 56 Kbps are even more whizzy!

Some computers have modems ready built and installed inside them. Others have modems that slide into a slot in the side of the machine.

The last but essential piece of equipment is a telephone line into which you plug your modem. You may have to move your computer to do this. When you are connected to the Internet, or 'online', your phone line will be busy and anyone who tries to call you will get an engaged tone.

If you've been trying to phone someone for hours on end and their phone is constantly engaged – guess what they are doing! People who spend a lot of time online sometimes get an extra telephone line put in, so that they can use the Internet at the same time as making and receiving phone calls.

Technical terms explained

Computer jargon can be very confusing and difficult to understand, but luckily there's a Glossary on page 123 which explains what all the technical terms used in this book mean.

Making the connection

So, you've got all of the basic hardware for connecting to the Net. What else do you need?

You need a subscription to an 'Internet access provider' or IAP. An IAP is a company which is connected to the Internet all the time. You pay a monthly fee to link into this connection.

When you begin the procedure for connecting to the Internet ('logging on'), you instruct your computer to tell your modem to make a phone call ('dial up') to your IAP. This opens the link between you and your IAP. The IAP then handles the link between it and the wider Internet.

There are hundreds of different Internet access providers. You will find the names and phone numbers of some them on page 122.

Online service providers are slightly different from Internet access providers. They allow you to use the Internet in the same way but they also give you access to additional 'online content' – electronic information only *they* provide, for example up-to-the-minute news bulletins, or easy access to information about your favourite hobby.

You will find the names and phone numbers of major online service providers such as CompuServe and AOL on page 122.

Money, money, money

Like most hobbies, using the Internet can be expensive, so it's important that you have a rough idea of the basic costs.

Most IAPs charge a monthly subscription fee which gives you free, unlimited access to the Internet, although some IAPs also charge a one-off fee when you first open an account with them.

You also have to pay the telephone company for the time you spend online, but the good news is that your IAP is only a local call away so you always pay local phone rates.

Online service providers tend to have a cheaper monthly subscription fee, which gives you free access to the Internet and the additional online content, but for a limited time each month. Once you have used up this time, you are charged by the hour for the time you spend online. This is on top of your phone bill.

What software do I need?

EVERYTHING YOU NEED TO CONNECT TO THE INTERNET

To write and send electronic messages and to receive email from other people, your computer needs some instructions. You get this from email software. To get access to all the information on the World Wide Web, you will need a 'Web browser'. The World Wide Web is a sort of storage system for the data held on computers connected to the Internet.

Luckily, most IAPs provide both these programs along with details about how to install them, but check that yours does before signing up.

Your IAP may supply other software with strange names such as FTP, Gopher and Telnet, but in this book we're going to concentrate on getting to grips with email and Web browsing packages.

17

Getting set up

Like anything to do with
computers, setting up your
Internet connection can
be a complicated and
frustrating process.
Good luck!

First, plug the various
bits of equipment
together. Then
follow the
instructions in
your manual to get
your computer and
your modem talking to each other.

Then insert the disk or CD-ROM from your IAP and
follow the on-screen instructions. With any luck, this
will get you online!

Choosing an IAP

*When you choose an IAP, check what kind of help it
offers to its customers. Does it have a friendly telephone
helpline and, if so, is it open in the evenings and at
weekends when you are most likely to be wrestling with
the various bits of your computer?*

*Cover disks on Internet magazines often allow you to
try out an IAP free for a month. But sometimes you will
have to ask an adult to give their credit card number
before you can use them. Always remember to stop the
payment if you decide not to continue using the service
after the free trial.*

3 | All about email

**Email addresses • Sending email •
Replying to a message • Email
activities • Fun stuff • Online safety**

Right, that's a lot of the dull but necessary technical stuff over and done with – now you're ready to start doing things on the Net.

What's great about electronic mail (or 'email' for short) is that it's much faster than the postal service, and it doesn't have to fight with the dog to deliver your letters! Internet users call ordinary letter post 'snail mail' because it's so unbelievably slow!

Email is also a lot cheaper than a telephone call or the postal service, especially if you're sending a message to someone on the other side of the world – and you don't have to remember to buy stamps!

To send an email to someone you must know their email address, which probably means you'll have to phone and ask them for it. Make sure you write it down carefully.

A smart address

Of course, to communicate with other Internet users, you also need your own email address. All email addresses have basically the same format and look something like this:

richard@any-iap.co.uk

OK, it looks like mumbo jumbo but you'll soon learn to read the code.

All email addresses start with the name of the user, in other words – you. Then there is an @ symbol which stands for 'at'. Next comes the name of the 'host', the organisation which holds your email for you. This will probably be your IAP. The 'domain type', describes the host. In this case, **co** tells you that the host is a company. Finally there's a country code – **uk** obviously stands for United Kingdom. The different parts are separated by full stops, called dots if you're reading an email address out to someone.

Decoding email addresses

DOMAIN TYPES

co.uk	UK company
com	US or global company
edu	Educational institution
gov	Government body
org	Charity
sch.uk	UK school

COUNTRY CODES

au	Australia
ca	Canada
fr	France
nz	New Zealand
uk	United Kingdom

If an email address doesn't have a country code, it's probably in the USA.

When you sign up with an IAP, you will automatically get an email address. Most of this will be fixed because your messages must go to your IAP's computer before they are forwarded on to your computer, but you can choose the part before the @ symbol.

You need to think of a user name before you sign up. You can go for your real name or something completely silly – anything as long as you can remember it! Some names may already be taken, so have a few different options ready.

Sending a test email

There are several different email packages around (Eudora and Microsoft Mail are popular ones) but they all work in similar ways. If you follow these general instructions you won't go too far wrong.

1 First, log on to the Net and load up your email software.

2 Then open a new email document – this is like picking up a blank piece of paper. Most email software automatically inserts your address as the sender's address.

3 In the header at the top of the document, type in the address of the 'recipient', the person you are sending the message to. It's very important that you type this address accurately. If you don't, your message won't be delivered. If you don't know anyone who has email yet... send a message to yourself!

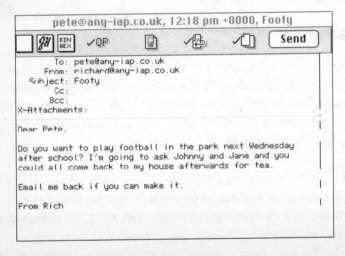

```
  pete@any-iap.co.uk, 12:18 pm +0000, Footy
 ┌──┐┌───┐         ┌─┐      ┌──┐  ┌──────┐
 │94││BIN│ ✓QP     │ │ ✓╞▭  │  │  │ Send │
 └──┘│HEX│         └─┘      └──┘  └──────┘
          To: pete@any-iap.co.uk
        From: richard@any-iap.co.uk
     Subject: Footy
          Cc:
         Bcc:
 X-Attachments:

 Dear Pete,

 Do you want to play football in the park next Wednesday
 after school? I'm going to ask Johnny and Jane and you
 could all come back to my house afterwards for tea.

 Email me back if you can make it.

 From Rich
```

4 Fill in the 'subject line' with a short description of what the message is about, for instance 'Test message' or 'Hi!'

5 Type your message in the empty space below the 'header'. As this is a test message, make sure you ask the recipient to reply as soon as possible, so that you know they've received it.

6 When you've finished, instruct the email software to send your message. You usually do this by clicking on a Send button.

7 Your email is now winging its way to the recipient. Most of the time email arrives within minutes but sometimes it can take a few hours to reach its destination – it depends how much other 'traffic' there is on the Internet. If the recipient isn't online, your email is stored safely until they log on and check their mail.

8 You are unlikely to get an immediate reply so log off for now. To check whether you've got a message, log on again a little later and ask your software to check the mail.

One of the most exciting things about email is that it's as quick and easy to communicate with people on the other side of the world as people just over the road.

If you have a brother or sister who is away at college they will have an email address. Relatives and friends who live abroad may have one, too. Most companies and organisations also have email so it's a good way to contact them for information.

However, it's expensive to stay online for long periods of time so the sensible thing to do is to write and read your messages when you're 'offline' – not connected to the Net. It goes like this: log on – check your mail – log off – now read your mail and write your replies – log on again – send your replies (maybe check your mail again just in case!) – log off – and so on...

Sending a reply

To reply to a message, give your software an instruction
via the menu or hit the Reply button. This will open a new
document. The header will have your address and the
address of the recipient filled in and the subject line will
be the same as the original message.

Most email software will 'quote' the original message in
your reply. This means it appears automatically. Each line
usually starts with a > symbol or tag. You can then insert
comments or delete sections.

Netiquette

*Although there are no rules on the Internet, Net users
have developed a set of customs for how to behave.
This is called 'Netiquette' ('Internet' + 'etiquette'). For
example, it's polite to reply promptly to an email, even
if you just say you've got the message and will answer
properly later.*

What you can do with email

When you've mastered the basics of sending, receiving and replying to email, you can start exploring the features of your software. You may not have all these features but you should find some of them.

Signature files

A signature file, once you've created it, will appear at the bottom of all your emails. It's a great way of personalising your messages. Some people include a brief description of who they are, or a joke, or piece of text that they like. Others create wacky and imaginative pictures using keyboard characters (you may have to squint to see what they are!). Keep people interested by changing your signature file regularly.

```
              (    )
            ~(^^^)~
             ) @@ \~_          |\
            /   | \           \~ /
           ( 0  0 ) \          | |      Hey
           --___/~ \           | |      Hiya
           /'__/ |  ~-_____/ |        Doin?
   o      _  ~---~    ___---~
     O    //   |      |
          ((~\ _|        -|
    o  O //-_ \/ |     ~ |
        ^  \_ /       ~ |
           |        ~ |
           |  /    ~ |
           |  (      |
           \   \      /\
          / -_____-\  \ ~~-*
          | /       \ \    .==.
           / /        / /     | |
          /~ |      //~ |     |_|
```

Nicknames

If your software has an address book, you can use this to store addresses that you use frequently. This means that you don't have to type them in each time. You may also be able to use 'nicknames', so if you want to send a message to **richard@any-iap.co.uk,** you can just type in Rich and the software will know who you mean.

By the letter

Email users love abbreviations and acronyms, where letters stand for whole phrases, because they're quicker to type and fun to use. Here are some of the most common ones. Why not start using them in your messages? Or make up some new ones of your own?

INTERNET ABBREVIATIONS

BTW	By the way
IMO	In my opinion
IMHO	In my humble opinion (usually meant sarcastically)
SWIM?	See what I mean?
<G>	Grin
IRL	In real life (i.e. not on the Net)
F2F	Face to face (i.e. not on the Net)
BCNU	Be seeing you
CUL	See you later
TNX	Thanks

Attachments

With most email software you can't do fancy things like putting words in bold or centring them like you can in a word processor program. And even if you can, to see the document exactly as you've typed it, the person at the other end must have the same software. However, you may be able to 'attach' documents. This is like paper-clipping another document to your email. You can attach text and image files like this. This is a very fast way to send documents, and they come out at the other end looking exactly the same as you sent them.

'Live' Web addresses

If you and a friend both have recent versions of the same email software, you can put the address of a place on the World Wide Web that you want them to visit in the main part of your message. If they read it while they are online and have a Web browser open, they can just click on the Web address to go straight to it.

Tips on tidiness

Every so often you should go through your mailboxes and delete all the messages you don't want anymore. Otherwise the memory in your computer will eventually get used up. Some email software saves copies of all the messages you send, too, so give this a spring clean from time to time as well. If there are some you want to save, you can always print them out and keep a 'hard' or paper copy.

You will have an Inbox, where incoming mail arrives, and an Outbox, where messages waiting to be sent are stored. However, if you have the option it's a good idea to file your messages. You may be able to set up separate mailboxes where you can keep emails from a particular friend or about a particular topic.

Show your feelings

Typing an email to someone isn't quite the same as having a conversation with them or even talking to them on the phone because the person you're writing to can't see your face or hear your voice, so they can't tell how you're feeling. Of course you can write it out in words – 'I am happy' – but Internet users have developed a shorthand language which communicates emotions via the keyboard.

'Emoticons', also called 'smileys', are little pictures put together from punctuation marks and letters which show how you're feeling. Here are some of the most common ones. It helps if you look at them sideways! Keep a look out for others, or why not try inventing your own?

Emoticons

:-)	Happy
:-))	Very happy
:-(	Sad
:'-(	Crying
:-D	Laughing out loud
:-O	Surprised
:-ø	Bored
;-)	Winking
:-/	Undecided
:-&	Tongue-tied
:-P	Sticking out tongue
{}	Hug
:-# or :-*	Kiss

Safety first

Just like the real world, the Internet can be a dangerous place, so it makes sense to take some simple precautions to protect yourself.

You don't have to tell the truth in an email – no one will know if you don't – but that means other people can lie, too. Remember that the people you contact online are not always who they seem, and that includes people who become email penfriends or 'keypals'.

Treat others in the same way as you would like to be treated. However, if you get email from a stranger, don't feel you have to answer it, and if anything in an email upsets you in any way, tell an adult.

Be careful about what information you give out, particularly to strangers. Don't email details of where you live, your telephone number or when you're going on holiday to anyone you don't know in real life.

Finally, remember that email is private communication. If you're accessing the Internet from someone else's computer they may not want you to 'borrow' their email address.

On the other hand, you may be able to set up a mailbox for yourself on their machine or, if you can access the Web (see chapter 4), you can get a free email address from a company called Hotmail:
http://www.hotmail.com

4 | The wonderful World Wide Web

The World Wide Web • Browsers • Logging on to a Web site • Web addresses • Hyperlinks • Solving access problems

The Internet has existed since the 1960s, when it was set up by the US Army to be a network that could be used during or after a nuclear attack! However, the real explosion of interest in the Internet happened more recently, in the early 1990s, when the 'World Wide Web' (or 'Web' for short) was invented.

If you're afraid of spiders, don't worry because the Web is nothing to do with them. It's a way of looking at the information which is held on the millions of large 'host' computers that make up the Internet. It provides a method of viewing and interacting with that information, whether it's text, images or sounds.

It's quite difficult to describe exactly what the Web is.
The best way to understand it is, of course, to see for
yourself. If you read on and follow the instructions, you
can do just that.

The chances are your IAP will have given you a browser
called either Microsoft Internet Explorer or Netscape
Navigator. There are others but these are the big ones.
Both work in broadly the same way, although some of
their features are different.

We can come back to the finer points of browsers later
but for now we're going to jump straight in and access
a Web site.

Accessing a Web site

1 First, log on to the Net and load up your browser.

2 If you're using Netscape Navigator, click on the button marked Open on the toolbar at the top of the screen. In the box that appears, type:
http://www.ex.ac.uk/bugclub/
Make sure you get this exactly right.

3 If you're using Microsoft Internet Explorer, click in the Location box on the toolbar at the top of the screen and type in: **http://www.ex.ac.uk/bugclub/**
Again, make sure you get this exactly right.

4 Then press the Return key on your keyboard, take a deep breath and wait patiently for several moments.

5 If you see words and pictures gradually swimming into view you've done it! Welcome to the Web – you can now call yourself a Nethead!

This is the Bug Club Web site for people who are fascinated by everything to do with insects and it should look something like this:

A Web site is a collection of Web pages, held on one computer anywhere in the world. There are millions of Web sites to choose from. This one has been picked more or less at random so don't worry if insects make your flesh creep!

One of the best things about the Web is that it can be much more up-to-date than any book. Because things change all the time you may not have exactly the same picture as this one, but don't worry about that.

If you can't see anything, try going back and typing in the Web address again. Include all the full stops but don't put a full stop at the end. Mis-typing an address is a very common error. If you've tried this and still can't see anything, turn to the section on trouble-shooting on page 44.

Every individual computer and every single page on the Internet has a separate identity – it's own address. Get that address wrong and you'll end up in the wrong place or, more likely, nowhere at all in cyber-outerspace...

How Web addresses work

Web addresses are made up in a similar way to email addresses but the first part is usually **http://** which stands for hypertext transfer protocol. This is a reminder to your browser that you are accessing data on the Internet. However, you don't usually need to worry about this as most browsers are clever enough to work it out for themselves and will automatically put in the **http://** part.

The second part of a Web address is almost always **www** and you don't need to be a genius to work out that this stands for World Wide Web.

Like email addresses, this is usually followed by the name of the organisation or company which hosts or runs the Web pages, or simply the name of the site, and then a domain type and a country code. Sometimes you also have to give a file name – such as **index.htm** – as well as the domain name.

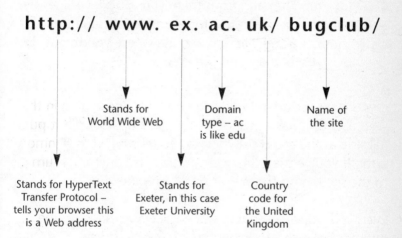

http:// www. ex. ac. uk/ bugclub/

Stands for
World Wide Web

Domain
type – ac
is like edu

Name of
the site

Stands for HyperText
Transfer Protocol –
tells your browser this
is a Web address

Stands for
Exeter, in this case
Exeter University

Country
code for
the United
Kingdom

Born in the USA

Because the Internet was invented in the United States, American organisations don't have to put a country code in their Web and email addresses. That's why a lot of addresses just end in **com**.

Hopping around

Right, let's go back to the Bug Club Web site. If you look at your computer screen you'll see that some of the words are underlined. This is a clue that things are not all they might seem.

Using the Web isn't like reading a story book, where you need to start at the beginning and read on until the end for the story to make sense. Using the Web is more like using an encyclopedia. You can start wherever you want (the Bug Club Site) and from there you can move sideways to lots of other related sites (for example 'Museums and insectariums'). You never know quite where you might end up as you hop around the Web...

The underlined words are what's known as 'hyperlinks' or just 'links'. If you use your mouse to click on one of these, it will take you somewhere else – another picture, another page or even another Web site altogether.

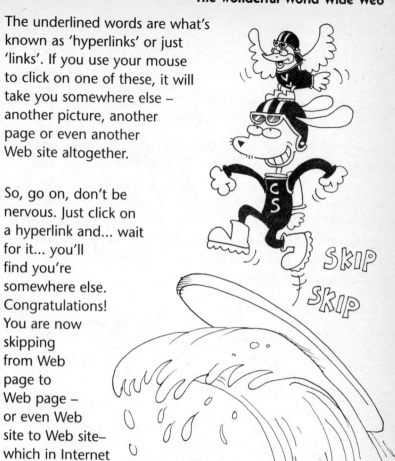

So, go on, don't be nervous. Just click on a hyperlink and... wait for it... you'll find you're somewhere else. Congratulations! You are now skipping from Web page to Web page – or even Web site to Web site– which in Internet jargon is called 'surfing the Web'.

If words appear in different colours from the main text they are usually hyperlinks. Sometimes your cursor changes when you hit a hyperlink. Static and flashing graphics can also hide hyperlinks. If you've used CD-ROMs you will already be familiar with this idea but even if you haven't you'll soon learn to spot a hyperlink.

The wonderful World Wide Web

Even if insects are not your thing, spend some time looking at the Bug Club Web site because this will give you an idea of what Web sites are like.

You'll see that the screen is divided up into two 'frames'. What you see in the larger, right-hand frame changes depending on where you go in the site. The narrow, left-hand frame lists the Bug Club's different areas. It stays there wherever you are in the site.

If, after surfing around the site, you want to go back to the first page or 'home page', then click on the top button in the left-hand frame, marked 'The Bug Club'.

Older browsers can't handle frames. If yours can't, click on the 'No frames' link if there is one and you'll get a different view.

Explore the Bug Club site and you should be able to find details of the club's newsletter, plus some articles from past issues. Look for the information on keeping insects as pets and see if you can find the penpals area. This lists the addresses of people who want to swap email about insects with fellow fanatics.

You'll almost certainly see a hyperlink on the word 'FAQ', too. This stands for 'frequently asked questions' and it's an abbreviation you will come across everywhere on the Internet.

FAQ documents give the answers to the questions that first-time visitors and 'newbies' or beginners always ask. If you want to know something about the Bug Club, it's probably in the FAQ.

Trouble-shooting

If you're having trouble accessing the Bug Club or any other Web site, you'll get an 'error message' which gives you some idea about what the problem is.

Check you've typed in the address correctly. Are the full stops in the right place? There's no full stop on the end is there? Whenever you input an address, follow the capital and small letters carefully. Web addresses are 'case sensitive' so it does matter whether you use capital or small letters.

The Web isn't perfect – sometimes it goes wrong. However, there are people who can help. Web sites often have an email address at the bottom of the first page for a Webmaster. And if you have repeated problems connecting to the Web, contact your IAP because either you or it may have a technical problem.

The wording may be slightly different but here are some of the most common error messages you'll come across.

Unable to locate host

This appears for a variety of reasons. First, check the address carefully, but if you're sure you've got it right you may find that you are able to log on by simply accessing the page again.

Network connection refused by server

This means the site is very popular and too many people are trying to access it at the moment. If this happens a couple of times in a row, go somewhere else instead and try again later.

Not found

This means the page has probably moved to another place or been deleted. If there's a link to the new address click on it. Or try just typing the domain name – for example, **www.ex.ac.uk** for the Bug Club. This will take you to the first ('home') page of the site and you may be able to find the page you want from there.

5 | Travels in cyberspace

Join a children's community • Read all about it • Meet a world figure • Send a postcard • Have a laugh • Fun stuff

OK, this is where it gets really exciting because now you're going to look at a few more sites to give you an idea of the range of stuff you can see and do on the Web.

For each site you'll find a name, Web address and a short description. Of course you don't have to look at everything mentioned in this book, but if something takes your interest, why not give it a whirl?

Places just for you

KIDS' SPACE
http://www.kids-space.org/

Kids' Space is exactly what it says it is – an online area designed especially for anyone under the age of 16. There are loads of things you can do there and it's well worth a visit.

Kids' Space is an electronic environment for sharing your creative work with other people. In the Kids' Gallery you can display your own art. You can send your stories to StoryBook and at the Beanstalk Project you can help create an online picture book by sending either a picture or a story to go with someone else's work. Kids' Space also has an area for sound files of music recorded by children. Start by exploring the things other people have contributed.

The FAQs on using the Internet and making the most of Kids' Space are very good and you'll also come across a character called Guide Bear, who will help you out if you get stuck. What's great about Kids' Space is that it's about doing, not just looking.

Same but different

If you can't get on to Kids' Space, here is a list of similar places you can try visiting. They all have slightly different personalities so find the one where you feel most at home.

CYBERKIDS
http://www.cyberkids.com/
Another spot for stories, pictures and sounds. Contributions welcome.

KIDSCOM
http://www.kidscom.com/
Games, craft ideas and a graffiti wall.

Strange symbols

It can't be said too often – always type Web addresses carefully making sure that any slash symbols are facing forward like this: /.

In some addresses you'll see a symbol which looks like this: ~. It's called a 'tilde'. You may have to search your keyboard to find it but it will be there somewhere.

THE LOOKING GLASS GAZETTE

http://www.cowboy.net/~mharper/LGG.html

A showcase for all sorts of creative work by kids.
Again, you can send in your own.

PLANET ZOOM

http://www.planetzoom.com/

Illustrated stories written by children. You can be
published here, too.

OZ KIDZ INTERNAUT CYBER CENTRE

http://www.gil.com.au/ozkidz/index.html

It comes from down under but it's not just for Australians.

Registration time

*Some Web sites like to know who their users are,
so before you can access all areas, you may have to
register. This usually means filling in a form with your
name, email address and a password. If you choose
the same password each time you register at a new
site, you'll be less likely to forget it! But don't use a
password that needs to be kept secret (such as your
Internet account details).*

Online magazines

TOO COOL FOR GROWNUPS
http://www.tcfg.com/

Some sites on the Web are called 'ezines', which is short for 'electronic magazines'. Like paper publications they have lots of different features and their pages change frequently, usually once a month but sometimes more often. However, unlike their 'dead tree' relations they are interactive and there are things to do as well as read.

Too Cool For Grownups is an ezine for kids about the Web itself and if you follow the links you'll be taken all over the Net. In the Too Cool Zone you'll find links to TCFG's Top Ten Web Sites, tried and tested by people your age with the same kind of interests as you. You can also cast your vote for what's hot and what's not.

Same but different

Just as in any newsagents, there are all sorts of different ezines available on the Web. Here is a tiny selection:

LITTLE PLANET TIMES
http://littleplanettimes.com/
A newspaper for
kids and by kids.

PATHFINDER – TIME FOR KIDS
http://www.pathfinder.com/@@1XMVagUALRnUno@n/TFK/
An American service featuring news about current events
relevant to young people.

YAKITY YAK
http://www.myfavoriteco.com/zeen.html
A chatty ezine with a colourful bunch of characters.

And the winner is...

*Many sites run competitions with fantastic
prizes but before you try your luck, check
the rules. If, for example, the site is run
from the US, only people who live in America
may be allowed to enter. This is usually because
the prizes have to be posted by snail mail.*

Through the keyhole

WELCOME TO THE WHITE HOUSE FOR KIDS
http://www.whitehouse.gov/WH/kids/
html/kidshome.html

This is one of the most famous sites on the Internet. It's an online guided tour of the White House, the home of the President of the United States, and it's given by Socks, the White House cat. Even if you're not an American citizen, you'll find this site interesting and fun.

The tour takes you through the history of the White House and tells you about the President and all the other people and animals that live in the White House.

You can even send an email to the President, the Vice President or the First Lady (the President's wife). Include your own address and you're guaranteed to get a reply!

Same but different

THE BRITISH MONARCHY
http://www.royal.gov.uk/

At the official Web site of the British royal family you can't email the Queen herself – but you can sign her visitors' book.

Commercial breaks

As you surf, you'll notice that some Web pages have advertisements at the top. These ads often flash, encouraging you to click on them to find out more information about the product that's being advertised. It's up to you whether you click or not.

Ads or 'banners' can be annoying because they slow down the speed at which pages load. However, the people who run the site charge companies money for these ads, which is how the sites are paid for. This means you can access the sites for free.

Postcard pleasures

The Electric Postcard
http://postcards.www.media.mit.edu/Postcards/

If you fancy sending something a little bit more colourful than an ordinary email, visit the Electric Postcard Web site and send a postcard instead.

The pictures range from famous works of art to moody black and white photographs. Choose the one you like, write your message and send it off. The person you've sent it to will get an email telling them that a card has arrived and giving them instructions on how to pick it up.

Over two million cards have been sent using this great, free service. Why not log on and give it a go?

Same but different

AWESOME CYBER CARDS
http://www.marlo.com/card.htm
As well as postcards, you'll find a wide range of birthday and valentine cards here.

Laugh? I almost did!

KIDS' JOKES
http://megascene.ukonline.co.uk/jokes.html
Netheads love truly awful jokes and there are hundreds of jokes pages on the Web. If the ones at this site don't make you chuckle, why not fill in the form and send in your own favourite? The best (or worst!) are selected to appear online.

Same but different

JOKE ZONE
http://www.owl.on.ca/owl/joke.html
Riddles, knock knock jokes and the 'groan phone'.

Silly season

COUNTDOWN
http://www.spiders.com/cgi-bin/countdown/

OK, this site is pretty pointless really but it's also quite fun – at least for a few minutes. What it does is calculate – to the very last second – the amount of time between two events, so if you want to know how long you've been alive or how long it is until your birthday, this nifty little page will work it out for you. However, make sure you follow the instructions carefully and use the right format for the date and time.

Same but different

MADLIBS MALL
http://www.connect-time.com/dec96/madlibs.html
Type in words at random and let the computer do the hard work – it will write an extremely daft story for you.

Other sites just for you

CARLOS' COLORING BOOK
http://coloring.com/
Throw away your felt-tips
and use your computer
to colour in the
on-screen
pictures.

ILLUSIONWORKS
http://www.illusionworks.com/
An amazing collection of online optical illusions, including
illusions you can hear!

PEG GAME
http://www.bu.edu/htbin/pegs/
Playing this simple but fun game against the computer will
test your powers of concentration.

STAGE HAND PUPPETS
http://fox.nstn.ca/~puppets/activity.html
Oh yes! How to dress up a paper bag or give a sock a
fresh look.

STRING FIGURES FROM AROUND THE WORLD
http://itpubs.ucdavis.edu/richard/string
Get in a tangle at home by following these step-by-step
instructions for making patterns and objects out of string.

More about browsers

Buttons • Loading images • Bookmarking favourite sites • Home pages • Protect yourself

You've learnt quite a lot about the Web already, but now you're going to brush up your browser know-how find out some useful tricks to help you improve your surfing technique.

Your browser window

Toolbar
Buttons that do nifty things and help you move around the Web are here

Address box
Shows the address of where you are on the Web at the moment

Activity icon
When this graphic is moving you know that something is happening

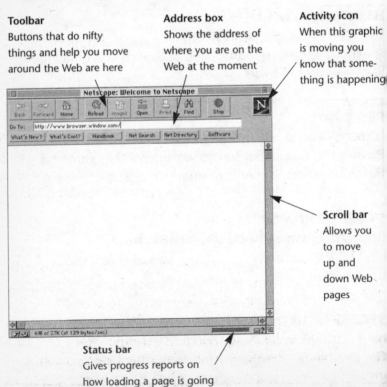

Scroll bar
Allows you to move up and down Web pages

Status bar
Gives progress reports on how loading a page is going

You're already a fairly experienced Web-wanderer, so you will probably have discovered several of these browser features for yourself, but here is a list and a brief description of what they do. To use any of these features, just click the button on the toolbar.

Back

This button takes you back to the last page you visited.

Forward

If you have moved back, this button takes you forward again.

Stop

This cancels the request to load a Web page. It's very useful if you click on a hyperlink accidentally or if you decide you don't want to look at something after all.

Reload or Refresh

If the transfer of data has been interrupted or the page hasn't loaded properly this button tells your browser to access it again. It is also useful on some sites where the page changes over time – click on Reload/Refresh to get the latest version.

In the picture

Graphics and pictures tend to be big files that use up a lot of memory and are slow to load, so you can tell your browser to load the text of a Web page first, before it loads the images.

You can also instruct it not to load images automatically at all. Instead you will get an icon or small graphic which shows where there is a picture. If you get curious and want to see that picture, either click on it or hit the Images button if your browser has one.

You can control how your browser handles images, and many other things, through its Preferences/Options menu. See if you can find this in your browser.

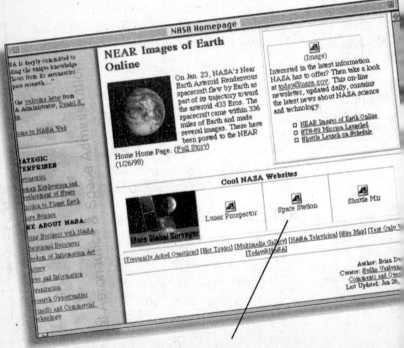

This shows that an image will load here shortly

Save your place

Let's face it, typing in Web addresses is boring, but by 'bookmarking' a site or making it a 'favourite' you can return to it time and time again without having to fumble over the keyboard. Look for the menu or button in your browser which allows you to do this.

Whenever you want to go to a particular site, find it in your list and simply click on it. Your computer has filed its address and will take you straight there.

Greedy browsers

New versions of Internet Explorer and Navigator are released every few months but the software eats up more and more space on your computer's hard disk and gobbles more and more memory, so many people don't upgrade and are quite happy using older versions of the software. This may mean that some Web pages do not display properly, and that some features are not available to you.

Home sweet home

You will already have come across the phrase 'home page'. It means the main page of a person or organisation's Web site but – and this is a bit confusing – it also means the page you first look at when you log on to the Web.

When you install your browser, the 'default' home page, or the home page that loads automatically, will probably be the site belonging to the company that produced your browser.

However, you're not stuck with this and it is really very easy to change it so that you see something you want to see whenever you go surfing. First you need to pick a site that you are happy to look at every time you log on.

This could be a site about something you're particularly interested in, a news service that changes every day, or just a picture that you find attractive. Check the address of the site and make a note of it.

Preferences: General

| **Appearance** | Colors | Fonts | Helpers | Images | Applications | Languages |

Toolbars

Show Toolbar as: ○ Pictures ○ Text ● Pictures and Text

Startup

On Startup Launch: ● Netscape Browser ○ Netscape Mail ○ Netscape News

Browser starts with:

   ○ Blank Page

   ● Home Page Location: `http://www.my.new.home.page.com/`

Link Styles

Links are: ☒ Underlined

Followed Links Expire: ○ Never ● After `30` days [**Now**]

[Cancel] [Apply] [OK ▶]

To change your home page, go to the Preferences or Options menu and type in the address of the page you want as your new home page. The Preferences menu is where you can personalise your browser so that it suits you.

To go back to your new home page at any time, click on the Home button on the toolbar. Don't forget – you can change your home page as often as you like.

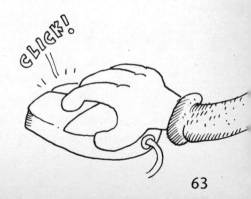

Here are some suggestions for cool home pages:

PURPLE MOON
http://www.purple-moon.com/
An online world created especially for girls.

THE SIMPSONS
http://www.foxnetwork.com/simpsons/simpson2.htm
Visit virtual Springfield, home to Bart and his family.

CARLINGNET
http://www.fa-premier.com/
For the footie crazy, everything there is to know about the
UK Premier League.

Invisible browsers

*If you are using an online service provider such as AOL
or CompuServe, Navigator or Internet Explorer may be
hidden behind the online service provider's own software,
but even though it has a slightly different appearance,
your browser will work in more or less the same way.*

Disappearing browsers

Microsoft has built Internet Explorer into the most recent version of its Windows operating system, the software that enables your computer to run, so in the future browsers probably won't exist as separate pieces of software at all.

And on a serious note

There's no getting away from it – if you look hard enough you can find a lot of unpleasant and upsetting material on the Web, stuff that young people, and most adults, find nasty and disturbing.

Unless you're deliberately looking for it you probably won't come across anything really horrible but just to be on the safe side, it's a good idea to ask an adult to install software which prevents your computer accessing this sort of site. Programs that do this include Cyberpatrol, Netnanny or Netsurf. Newer versions of Internet Explorer have a built-in feature which allows you to screen out sites you don't want to look at. You should be able to find this under ratings in Preferences. Doing this really does make sense.

More about browsers

It's important not to believe everything you read and see on the Web. Be smart and you'll soon sniff out what's true and what's not!

The best view

You will often see phrases such as 'Best viewed in Netscape Navigator 2' or 'Site optimised for Internet Explorer 3' on Web pages. This means that to be able to look at the site properly you need a particular version of Navigator or Internet Explorer. However, if you have a different browser the site may still work, or you can probably download the recommended browser there and then (see Chapter 8 for details on how to do this).

Look it up

Internet directories • Search engines • Other sites • Find it fast • Tips for searching

If you hop from Web site to Web site following links you'll certainly come across some interesting stuff. However, there are millions and millions of pages on the Net and if you're looking for something special you won't come across it by chance unless you're very lucky. That's why there are lots of places on the Web to help you find exactly what you want.

Directory enquiries

Internet directories are lists of Web sites and their addresses, arranged under different subject headings. Yahooligans is a good example of an Internet directory which collects together information about sites for young people. Start by logging on to the Yahooligans Web site:

http://www.yahooligans.com/

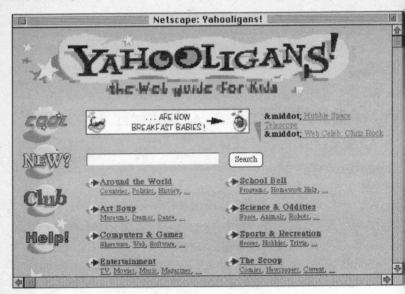

Scroll half way down the Yahooligans home page and you'll see a number of headings such as Around the World and Entertainment. Say you want to find out about mountain biking. You need to find a heading which relates to your chosen subject. Sports and Recreation sounds promising – so click on it.

This takes you to another, more detailed list of topics related to sport. Find Biking in the list and click on that. The next page is a shorter but more specialised list and it gives you two options: Mountain Biking and Tour de France. The number in brackets beside each of these headings is the number of Web sites you'll find listed under it.

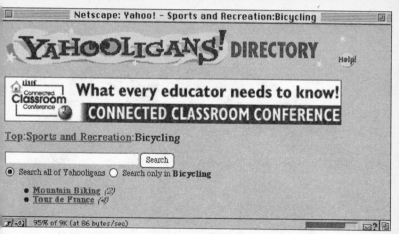

From this you can tell that there are two mountain biking sites. One is for GT Bicycles, the company which makes BMX bikes, and the other is for the Mountain Bike Network. Click and you can access either of them.

The Mountain Bike Network site has lots of information on different types of bike and if you find it useful and interesting you might want to bookmark it or make it a favourite.

However, if you forget to do this but want to go back to it at another time, you can log on to the Yahooligans home page but instead of going through the directory listings you can use something called a 'search engine' to search for it.

Search party

At the top of the Yahooligans home page, just underneath the Yahooligans logo and the New and Cool buttons, you'll notice that there is an empty 'query box' with the word Search next to it. Type 'Mountain Bike Network' into this box, click on the Search button and your site will be found for you. Then click on the highlighted name to go straight to the site.

If you don't find what you're looking for the first time, you can type another keyword – a word which describes what you're looking for – or a short phrase into the query box and then click on the Next Search button. Sometimes you need to try different ways of saying the same thing. In this case you might try typing in 'cycling' or perhaps just 'bikes'.

Yahooligans only searches a limited, though still very large, number of sites – basically it only catalogues sites for young people – but there are lots of other search engines and most of these have the details of every single page on the Internet.

This is because they send out robot programs called crawlers, worms or bots which look at each page and note what it's about and where it's stored. They are constantly at work because new sites are being created all the time.

It's a good idea to try out a few search engines and decide which one you like best. They all work in more or less the same way. This is how you use one called Infoseek.

http://www.infoseek.com/

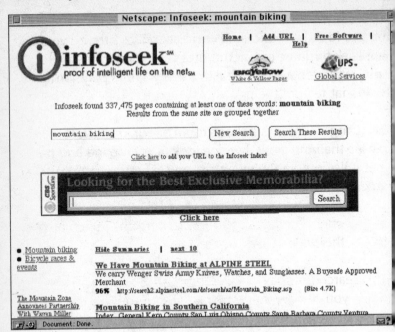

Searching by engine

To discover more sites about mountain biking, try typing the keywords 'mountain biking' into the Infoseek query box and then clicking on the Seek button.

Search engines are powered by very large computers and, amazingly, the results of your search come back in seconds. What you'll see is a list of titles with brief descriptions and addresses. The most relevant are at the top but it's a very long list, with 337,475 entries!

It would take weeks to check all these sites yourself, so make the search engine do it for you. Ask Infoseek to search the list for mountain bike sites in the UK by typing 'UK' into the box and then clicking on the Search These Results button. This time it comes up with 613 'hits' – fewer but still a lot.

That's how search engines basically work but smart surfers have a few clever tricks up their sleeves. What you've asked Infoseek to do is find all the sites that contain the word 'mountain' or the word 'biking'. What you really want is sites that feature the two words next to other.

Try using double quotation marks or put hyphens between words that you want to appear next to each other, for example "mountain biking" or mountain-biking. When you're using hyphens, make sure there aren't any extra spaces in-between the hyphen and the words. Different search engines may ask you to use different punctuation to get the same results.

This search produces 29,696 hits and when you narrow that down to sites in the UK, the number is 280, which is much easier to cope with!

Looking for a good home page?

Directories and search engines make really good home pages. For example, if you set your browser so that when you log on it loads up Yahooligans or Infoseek, you'll always be able to search for sites quickly and easily.

Same but different

ALTAVISTA
http://www.altavista.digital.com/
Searches 60 gigabytes of data in seconds.

EXCITE
http://www.excite.com/
Says it checks 50 million Web pages for you.

HOTBOT
http://www.hotbot.com/
It's got a silly name but knows what it's doing.

SEARCH.COM
http://www.search.com/
Access to several search engines from just one page.

YAHOO
http://www.yahoo.com/
Big brother to Yahooligans.

Look it up

Useful services   Query box   Search the Web   Download software

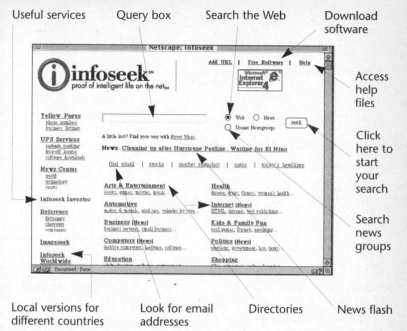

Access help files

Click here to start your search

Search news groups

Local versions for different countries   Look for email addresses   Directories   News flash

More tips for searching on Infoseek

- Make sure you get spellings rite (oops!).
- Try variations on words, for example CDROM and CD-ROM.
- Use capital letters for names and small letters for common words or phrases.
- Use a comma to separate people's names, otherwise Infoseek will look for someone called 'Bruce Willis Demi Moore' and won't find anyone.
- Don't forget that the most relevant sites appear first, so don't bother looking beyond the first 20 or so.
- Instead of just clicking on a hit, give your browser an instruction to open a new window so that you can flick easily between the site and the list.
- Several search engines have versions which only search sites in the UK or just Australian and New Zealand pages.
- Search engines are VERY, VERY USEFUL if you have a homework project to do!

8 | Jazz up your Web experience

Downloading software • Freeware and shareware • Plug-ins • Sound on the Web • Movement on the Web • Something called Java

One of the best things about the Internet is that you can use it to get free software. If you want a new version of a browser you can 'download' it, which means you connect to a Web site and give a command that transfers the program from the host computer to your computer.

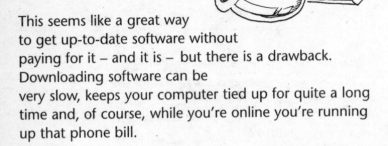

This seems like a great way to get up-to-date software without paying for it – and it is – but there is a drawback. Downloading software can be very slow, keeps your computer tied up for quite a long time and, of course, while you're online you're running up that phone bill.

You'll have noticed that there are places where you can download browsers all over the Net, but here are the sites for the companies that make them.

MICROSOFT
http://www.microsoft.com/

NETSCAPE
http://www.netscape.com/

'Mirror sites' are Web sites which have copies of the same software available for download. If you are offered a choice, opt for a server, a big computer which serves up information, in your part of the world.

Set your alarm clock

If you live in the UK, a good time to go online is early in the morning, preferably before breakfast, because there are a lot of Netheads in the USA and at that time they are safely tucked up in bed, so the Internet isn't too busy.

TIME ZONE CONVERTER
http://poisson.ecse.rpi.edu/cgi-bin/tzconvert
Check what time 7am Greenwich Mean Time is where you are.

Why are we waiting?

How long does it take to download a piece of software? Well, that's like asking how long is a piece of string? It's impossible to be exact because it depends on the size of the file you are downloading, how fast your modem is, and how busy the Internet is.

If the size of the file is measured in kilobytes then it's probably a matter of minutes, but if it's in megabytes you're going to have a long wait – perhaps up to an hour (yawn!).

Make sure you know what kind of computer you have so that you get the right version of the software. You may have to say where you want the software to be stored on your computer's hard disk. You will have to follow the installation instructions before you can run the new program.

Sometimes the software you download will work for a limited period of time, say a month, before 'expiring'. Then it will stop working and if you like it, you'll either have to buy it or download it again.

Don't break the law

Freeware is free to download and use. Shareware is free to download but after you've been using it for a while you must either register your copy and pay a small fee to the author or stop using it.

If you like a program, it's worth registering because you will then get access to technical help, extra features and upgrades. If you don't register, you could be breaking the law.

Be sure to read the 'software licence' which comes with all software and tells you how you're allowed to use it.

Plug yourself in

Plug-ins are extra pieces of software that work with your browser to give you access to additional features such as sound, video and 3D graphics.

If you're using recent versions of Navigator or Internet Explorer, the plug-ins you need may well be built in to the browser. If not, you can download them from the Net.

Popular plug-ins are:

REAL PLAYER
http://www.realaudio.com/
Gives you access to high-quality sound clips.

SHOCKWAVE
http://www.macromedia.com/Tools/Shockwave/
Another popular player which delivers animations that can be interactive.

QUICKTIME
http://www.quicktime.apple.com/
Use this to view video clips and mini 'movies'.

Tune in

One of the things that a plug-in such as Real Player allows you to do is hear and watch Webcasts – live events which are broadcast only on the Web – and to listen to the radio. OK, you could just turn on the real radio – but on a Web site you can access archives of old sound clips and you may be able to pick up real-time – in other words 'as it's broadcast' – stations in other parts of the world. Don't forget that you have to be online to listen – and that means running up your phone bill.

RADIO 1

http://www.bbc.co.uk/radio1/

VIRGIN RADIO
http://www.virginradio.co.uk/

CAPITAL RADIO
http://capitalfm.co.uk/

Get interactive!

Plug-ins make surfing the Web really exciting but they can take up a lot of hard disk space and memory.

Fun sites that use Shockwave:

CLEVERMEDIA SHOCKWAVE ARCADE GAMES
http://clevermedia.com/arcade/snowman.html
Including the Lava Lamp and the Snowman 2000 Construction Set.

WHERE'S WALDO? ON THE WEB
http://www.findwaldo.com/
It's up to you to find him.

ETCHY'S HOME PAGE
http://www.world-of-toys.com/
Puzzles, games and a screensaver.

Amazing sites which use Quicktime:

VOLCANO WORLD
http://volcano.und.nodak.edu/vw.html
Violent video clips of erupting volcanoes.

THE QUICKTIME ARCHIVE
http://film.softcenter.se/flics/long.html
Clips and trailers from all sorts of films.

Get hyperactive!

Plug-ins like Shockwave and Quicktime are programs
that are stored on your hard disk, but Java is a computer
language which downloads the software to run multimedia
– known as 'applets' – only when you need it.

Java is named after a type of coffee which is so strong it
makes you jump around and it's becoming very important
on the Web.

f a site needs Java, you must have a browser that can deal
with it. Most recent browsers are 'Java-enabled'.

Here is a site which will give you more information about
ava:

AVA HOME PAGE
ittp://www.javasoft.com/

9 | Chatting in cyberspace

Electronic noticeboards • Chat rooms • 3D worlds • More about safety

So you've sent email messages to all your friends and family who are online. But the Web also allows you to make new cyber-friends by communicating in other ways with people you don't already know.

One place you can do this is Cyberkids, which you may have visited already:
http://www.cyberkids.com/

In an area called Cyberkids Connection there are public electronic noticeboards where you can 'post' messages about all sorts of subjects, from music, movies and TV to homework. Within each section, there are different topics or 'threads'.

The way this works is that you send a message which appears on the noticeboard and then someone else sends one in reply, so over time a discussion develops.

This is great fun but it isn't instant. However, there are even more exciting places where you can talk to people via the keyboard and carry on a real conversation.

84

Let's have a chat

To have a real conversation you go to screen areas called 'chat rooms'. There are some on Cyberkids Connection. You do need a Java-enabled browser to use them and you must register first. However, once you've done that you enter a 'virtual space' where you can type messages to other kids and get replies in real time.

Keypals

On Cyberkids Connection there is a section for people who are looking for keypals. They post messages describing themselves and their interests. You can choose someone you like the sound of to write to. If you pick a keypal who lives in another part of the world it can be fascinating because their life is probably quite different from yours.

85

Chatting in cyberspace

In the Cyberkids chat rooms you can tell jokes, talk about your favourite bands, discuss what you're doing at the weekend – in fact what you chat about is up to you – and the responses appear on your screen at once. The people you are chatting to could be in the next town – or they could live on the other side of the world.

To take part, just type what you want to say in the message area and press the Return or Enter key. Your message will appear in the message display area along with other chatters' replies.

Teen talk

Only under 13s are allowed in Cyberkids Connection but if your older brother or sister is jealous of the kind of fun you're having online and wants to join in, send him or her to Cyberteens Connection.

Using the Cyberkids chat menus you can send a private message to one of the other people in the room or, if you're getting on particularly well, invite them into a private room for a one-to-one conversation.

VIRTUAL VIKKI
REQUESTING
ONE-TO-ONE
WITH CYBER
STEVE...

If you don't like someone, you can ignore them and fix it so that their messages don't come up on your screen. This is handy when another user is annoying you.

On the Internet, lots of people use nicknames rather than their real names, because it's more fun. A nickname can say something about you, for example what music you like, or it can give you a different online personality. You can give yourself a new nickname in the Cyberkids Connection chat rooms by using the menus.

Chatting in cyberspace

If you get your Internet access through an online service provider such as CompuServe or AOL, you will find that they have special areas where kids can chat, too. These work in a similar way to Cyberkids Connection.

Why register?

Registering is like joining a club and letting people know who you are. To register at a site you will need to give your name, a password and your email address. Each time you want to enter the site you have to log in with the same details, so don't forget that password!

Having to register is good because it means you often get up-to-date information about what's happening at a site by email. It also means that if someone in a chat room is bothering you the 'sysop' (the adult who keeps an eye on what's going on) can contact them directly and ask them to stop.

WATCHFUL EYE

Global chat

Another good place for meeting people and making friends
is Kidlink.
http://www.kidlink.org/

It's a space where young people can share their thoughts
and ideas about the world. Discussion is mainly in English
but there are areas for lots of other languages, including
Spanish and Japanese.

As well as real-time chat, there are email conversations
between groups and individuals and organised discussions
on specific topics. An adult 'moderator' checks what is said
and makes sure you stick to the point.

A different world

Of course when you chat on the Internet you can't see
the other person, but in 3D chat you choose a graphic
of a human figure to stand in for you in a virtual 3D
environment. This icon is called an 'avatar' and you use
it to interact with avatars belonging to other people.

Chatting in cyberspace

An organisation called Worlds was one of the first
to develop this sort of online experience and the 3D
environment on its Web site is an abandoned space station.
You look at this through the eyes of your avatar and your
view changes as you and your avatar move around it.

You can talk to everyone you meet by typing. There is also
a feature that allows you to 'whisper' private conversations.

You need special software to run Worlds and a free 'demo'
(demonstration version) can be downloaded from the
Worlds Web site. Be warned, it uses up a lot of hard disk
space and memory.

http://www.worlds.net

Staying safe

In all your communications with
other Internet users, you need
to be sensible and careful,
even if you're in a kids-only
space where there is a
sysop monitoring
what's happening.

Here are some guidelines
for staying safe online.

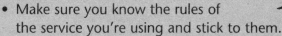

- Make sure you know the rules of
  the service you're using and stick to them.
- The Net has always been a very tolerant place
  so respect other users.
- The people you meet online have feelings, too,
  so remember that even though you can't see them,
  what you say can hurt them.
- Be patient with newbies and help if you can.
  After all, you were a beginner once, too.
- Never respond to someone who's bothering you.
  Ignore them, go somewhere else on the Web or log
  off altogether.
- If anything that happens online upsets you, tell the
  sysop or another adult immediately.
- It can be fun to try out a different personality but
  don't be afraid to be yourself online.
- Make sure you always know whether you are in a
  public area or having a private conversation.
- Never give out personal information, such as the
  address where you live or your telephone number,
  in public areas.

- Be very careful about giving out personal information in private conversations, too, even when you think you know someone well.
- Never meet friends you've made online in real life without an adult present.
- If you do meet an Internet friend, arrange the first meeting in a public place such as a café or park – it's safer and you need to know them better before you invite them to your home.
- Never give your password to anyone – not even to a sysop.
- Be aware of these guidelines but don't let them stop you having a great time!

If you or your parents would like more information about online safety, try the following places.

SAFEKIDS.ONLINE
http://www.safekids.com

RECREATIONAL SOFTWARE ADVISORY COUNCIL
http://www.rsac.org/

KID SAFETY
http://www.ou.edu/oupd/kidsafe/start.htm

10 Playing games online

**Action and adventure games •
Companies and products • More
about downloading • Shopping •
Online gaming • Brain teasers**

Many Internet users spend
a lot of time playing
games of one sort or another.
If you like games, the
Web has an enormous
amount to offer.

You now know enough
about how the Internet
works to find your own
way around, so in this
chapter there are a lot of
Web addresses and brief
descriptions of great places
to do with games, plus a
few tips.

Computer games

If you're into computers and the Internet there's a fairly
good chance you'll be into computer games. If so, then
you're in luck, because there are plenty of general games
sites which have up-to-date information on releases,
reviews and, best of all, demos.

Try out these places:

GAMES CENTER
http://www.gamecenter.com/
This site features reviews and lots of interesting articles
about the world of PC and console games.

GAMES DOMAIN
http://www.gamesdomain.co.uk/
Cheats, demos, downloads, freebies and detailed reviews.

GAMESPOT
http://gamespot.com/
Info on action and adventure games.

ELECTRIC PLAYGROUND
http://www.elecplay.com/
The speciality of this site is news about video games.

HAPPY PUPPY
http://happypuppy.com/
The Happy Puppy's paw print is all over this site, which is
excellent for freeware games.

Playing games online

If you've got a favourite computer games company it will definitely have a site on the Web. All you have to do to find its pages is carry out a search using a search engine.

Of course the games companies use their Web sites to advertise their products. They want you to persuade you to buy their games so they offer downloadable demos.

A demo of a game will probably expire after a certain time or, even more likely, it won't have all the features of the paid-for version, but in most cases it will still be perfectly playable and you'll be able to get a lot of enjoyment out of it.

Fox Interactive
http:/www.foxinteractive.com

Choose what you're going to download carefully because the software can take up a lot of space on your hard disk and downloading is quite time-consuming.

The software squeeze

Often, the files you download have been 'compressed' or squashed so that they use less space on the server and are quicker to download. This means that once they arrive on your computer, you have to 'decompress' or unsquash them.

You can tell whether a piece of software needs decompressing by the way its file name ends. For example, if a PC file name ends in **.zip** you need a program called WinZip to decompress it. If a Mac file ends in **.hqx** you can use a program called Stuffit Expander (also available for PCs).

Some files are 'self-extracting', which means that, once you've downloaded them, they decompress themselves automatically when you install them on your computer. PC files ending in **.exe** and Mac files ending in **.sea** are self-extracting.

There are lots of other sorts of compressed files and decompression programs to match them. You'll learn to recognise the different types and sometimes you just have to experiment to see what works.

This all sounds quite technical and difficult but don't worry because shareware versions of common decompression software can, of course, be found on the Net. The **Shareware.com** site is a good place to start searching.

http://www.shareware.com/

Shopping on the Web

Now, going back to demos, if you've played the trial version, liked it and want to buy the full game, you can of course go to a real-life computer games shop for it.

Or, on the other hand, at some Web sites you can visit the online store, get an adult to pay for it with a credit card and buy it over the Net.

Don't go down with a virus

If you're doing a lot of downloading, whether it's games or any other type of software, you should get hold of a virus checker program. A virus is a rogue program that can run riot in your computer, destroying data and generally causing trouble! Run the virus checker program regularly in case one of the files you download is infected with a computer virus. There are plenty of virus checkers available on the Net. Try **Shareware.com** *again.*

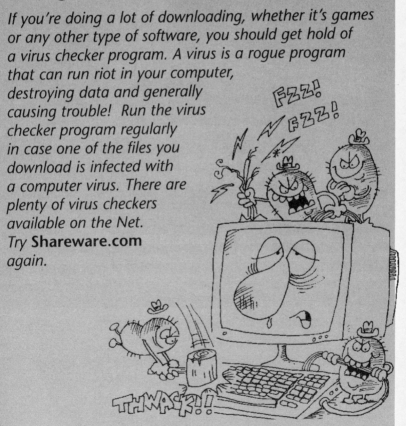

Playing games online

If you buy your games online you can sometimes download the full version there and then, but often the full package, complete with manual, is sent to you by snail mail.

In fact, via email order you can buy an enormous range of things without ever leaving the house – from flowers and food to CDs and clothes.

'Electronic commerce', as it's called, is becoming more and more popular but many people don't like the idea of sending the number of their credit card over the Net because their details could be stolen by a hacker (Internet criminal) and used illegally.

If you're going to shop at a Web site, make sure it's a 'secure server' that uses some form of 'encryption', a way of scrambling numbers and text so that they can't be decoded by the wrong people.

Play for real

Believe it or not, over the Net you can also play against real human opponents – modem to modem. This is called online gaming. You can play incredibly popular computer games such as Quake but you can also pit your wits in more traditional games such as chess. However, be warned that you do need a fairly powerful computer and a fast modem connection to do this. Otherwise you'll find you're always losing!

AVALON
http://www.avalon.co.uk/avalon/
A complicated and challenging multi-user, role-playing adventure game.

CHESSMASTER LIVE
http://www.chessmaster.com/
Chessmaster Live is an online chess game that lets you play chess against real people, all over the world, at any time of the day or night.

Whether you're a beginner or consider yourself quite an expert, you should be able to find an opponent with the same level of skill and experience.

DOOM PAGE
http://www.cis.ksu.edu/~trm/doom.html
This is a good place to find someone to play against and there's a link to an excellent Doom FAQ. Also, check out the list of the top ten ways to know whether Doom has taken over your life!

ID SOFTWARE
http://www.idsoftware.com/
Home to the makers of Doom, Quake and Duke Nukem but be warned that this site is very busy and it's often hard to get on to it.

A bit of peace and quiet

So far in this chapter we've mostly talked about computer games but if you don't like action and adventure games and you want a less violent way of entertaining yourself, the Web still has a lot for you. Here are some rather more peaceful places:

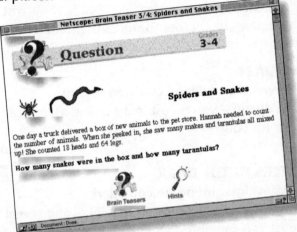

BRAIN TEASERS
http://www.eduplace.com/math/brain/
Every Wednesday, entertaining and mentally challenging puzzles appear on this Web site. The correct answers are posted the following week, along with new problems.

CONNECT 4
http://www.luc.ac.be/~hbaerten/vier/vierinit.html
Play the classic four-in-a-line game against the computer.

FAMILY GAMES
http://www.familygames.com/index.html
Specialising in non-violent computer games for all the family.

FORENSIC FILES

http://forensicfiles.bc.sympatico.ca/

Solve a mystery and travel the world with Newton the beagle.

GAMELAND

http://www.game-land.com/

Loads of smart little games, some of them for adults.

MANIC MAZE

http://www.worldvillage.com/maze.htm

It's not a dream – you're lost in an online maze. Can you find your way out???

MONSTERS IN THE DARK

http://www.imaginengine.com/dark/

A cute game – click to turn on the lights and reveal the monsters! You can also download a Mini Monster Making Kit and animate your own monsters.

11 Creating your own home page

The language of Web pages • How HTML works • The basic format • Common tags • Adding pictures • Creating a link • Shortcuts to a home page

The ultimate in Internet cool is having your own Web site. You might think that this is only for people who are very 'techy' but it's actually surprisingly easy.

Web pages are all written in a computer language called 'HTML', which stands for HyperText Markup Language. You might have noticed that addresses of some Web pages end in '**.html**' and this shows that they are files written in HTML.

Getting to grips with HTML seems very complicated at first but it isn't that difficult – if you can use a word processor you can do it.

Crack the computer code

HTML gives instructions to a browser about how text and pictures should appear on a Web page. It does this through a set of commands surrounded by the symbols < and > (the 'less than' and 'more than' keys on your keyboard). These commands are known as 'HTML tags'.

For example, <CENTER> (note the American spelling) tells a browser to place a piece of text in the centre of a Web page. Tags are almost always used in pairs, so each start tag is followed by a finish tag. In this case, the finish tag appears at the end of the text which you want centred. Finish tags always have the format </ >, so the HTML coding to centre a piece of text looks like this:

<CENTER>Hello and welcome to my Web page!</CENTER>

To get a clearer general idea of what we're talking about here, you can look at the HTML code of any Web page by using the menus in your browser to view the 'source' code. This will magically reveal the HTML which lies underneath what you see on screen.

```
http://www.ex.ac.uk/bugclub/

<HTML>
<HEAD>
   <TITLE>AES Bug Club Home Page</TITLE>
</HEAD>
<FRAMESET cols="100%" frameborders=0 border=0>
<NOFRAMES><BODY BGCOLOR="#FFFFFF" LINK="#0000A0" VLINK="#82A4B5">

<P>This page is designed to be viewed by a browser which supports
Netscape's Frames extension. This text will be shown by browsers
which do not support the Frames extension. Click
<A HREF="main.html">here</A> to enter the Bug Club Site (No Frames
Version). To view the site as intended by the Author get a decent
browser!! To the <A HREF="http://www.netscape.com">Netscape Site</A>.


</BODY>
</NOFRAMES>
   <FRAMESET cols="140,660" frameborders=0 border=0>
      <FRAME SRC="navig.html" name="navigation" NORESIZE
      scrolling="no" frameborder=0 borders=0 bgcolor="#ffffff">
      <FRAME SRC="main.html" name="right" NORESIZE
      frameborder=0 borders=0 bgcolor="#ffffff">
   </FRAMESET>
</FRAMESET>
</HTML>
```

Create your own Web page

All Web pages have a basic structure that you have to follow. It looks like this:

<HTML>

<HEAD> <TITLE> </TITLE> </HEAD>

<BODY>

</BODY>

</HTML>

A Web page should start and finish with a tag which shows it's written in HTML. To do this, you type <HTML> at the very top of your page and </HTML> as the very last thing on your page.

You put the name of your page – the description which appears on the bar at the top of the browser window – after the <HEAD> <TITLE> and before the </TITLE> </HEAD> tags.

Everything else on your page – all the text and pictures and the tags that give instructions on how these should look – go between the <BODY> and </BODY> tags.

Spot the tag

Here are some common HTML tags. Look at the source code of a Web page and see if you can spot them.

<B>This tag is for bold text.</B>

<I>This tag is for italic text.</I>

<CENTER>This tag centres the text.</CENTER>

<P>This tag starts a new paragraph and adds a space underneath that paragraph.</P>

<H1>This tag is for big headings.</H1>

<H3>This tag is for normal sized text.</H3>

<H5>This tag is for tiny text.</H5>

<BODYBGCOLOR="YELLOW">This tag makes the background colour of your page yellow.
</BODYBGCOLOR="YELLOW">
You don't need the <BODY></BODY > tag as well.

<IMG SRC="This tag places a picture – put the name of the file between these quotation marks.">

Creating your own home page

Let's look at the HTML code for a page which uses these tags:

```
<HTML>

<HEAD>

<TITLE>Mark's Home Page</TITLE>

</HEAD>

<BODY BGCOLOR="YELLOW">

<H1><CENTER>Hello and welcome to my Web page!
</CENTER></H1>

<H3><P>My name is <B>Mark.</B> I am 10 and I live in
Horsham in Sussex, England. My hobbies are cycling and
reading.</P>

<P>My favourite TV programmes are <I>Blue Peter</I>
and <I>Eastenders</I> and my favourite film at the
moment is <I>Hercules.</I></P>

<P> I love playing football. I am a goalie. I support Arsenal,
the greatest team in the world!</P>

<CENTER><IMG SRC="football.gif"></CENTER>

</H3>

<HR></HR>

<H5>I created this page in May 1998.</H5>

</BODY BGCOLOR="YELLOW">

</HTML>
```

This is how the same page looks when viewed in a browser.

Mark's Home Page

Hello and welcome to my Web page!

My name is Mark. I am 10 and I live in Horsham in Sussex, England. My hobbies are cycling and reading.

My favourite TV programmes are *Blue Peter* and *Eastenders* and my favourite film of all time is *101 Dalmations.*

I love playing football. I am a goalie. I support Arsenal, the greatest team in the world!

I created this page in May 1998.

In living colour

The background colour of this site is yellow. Most up-to-date browsers recognise HTML tags which describe background colours as 'RED', 'BLUE' and so on, but some older browsers only understand complicated codes for colours. For example, #00E4FF' is light blue. If a browser doesn't understand your colour coding, it will probably default to a grey background.

Great graphics

You'll know from your own surfing that pages with pictures
are far more interesting to look at than pages with just
text. Here's how to add a goofy graphic to your page to
make it quite clear that you are a *very* interesting person...

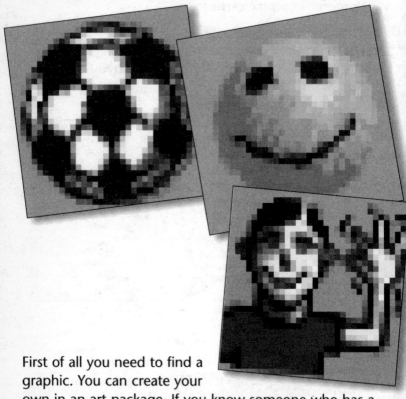

First of all you need to find a
graphic. You can create your
own in an art package. If you know someone who has a
scanner (a piece of equipment that turns a hard copy of a
picture into a digital file which can be understood by a
computer) you could ask them to scan in a piece of your
own artwork, or a photograph. It should be saved as a
.gif file.

However, the easiest way to get images is to search out
some clip art – free graphics that can be used by anyone.

Here are some places on the Web where you will find clip art:

CLIP ART UNIVERSE
http://www.nzwwa.com/mirror/clipart/
An excellent collection of signs and symbols – this is where Mark's football graphic came from.

ENCHANTED FOREST
http://www.geocities.com/EnchantedForest/
Backgrounds, buttons, bars and other graphics.

ICON MANIA
http://www.kidsdomain.com/icon/index.html
Some of these pictures are free, others are shareware so you pay the artist a small fee.

You save an image to your own computer's hard disk by clicking on it (or right-clicking on a PC) and using the menu that appears.

Images should be stored in the same place on your computer as you store your HTML document, so that a browser can find them easily.

Creating your own home page

It's polite to email people to let them know you're using their clip art, or to link to their site from your home page. To create a link, let's go back to Mark's home page.

Adding hyperlinks to other sites

Mark supports Arsenal Football Club, which has its own Web site. Mark wants everyone else to get excited about Arsenal too. He adds a hyperlink to his site so that visitors can go straight to the Arsenal pages:

http://www.arsenal.co.uk/

He can do this by adding some more HTML code:

<A HREF="http://www.arsenal.co.uk/">Arsenal</A>

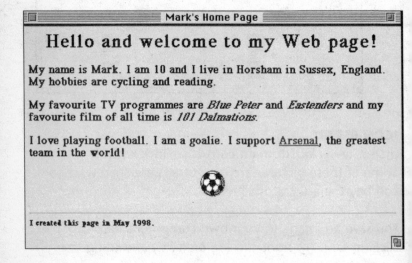

Be creative

You can create a home page about yourself – what you like, your favourite Web sites and so on, or you could create one about something you're interested in – a hobby or a club you belong to. Go on, open a new document in your word processor and start typing! Remember to save it as a text format file.

Don't break the copyright laws!

You must be very careful about where you take images from because most are 'copyright' and can't be used without the owner's permission. For example, you might want to brighten up your page with a graphic of Pooh Bear from the Disney Web site but don't do it – the picture belongs to Disney, not you, and you will be breaking the law if you use it.

A few tips

If you see something on a Web page that you like, you can open it in your browser and look at the source HTML code which lies underneath. Work out which section gives the instructions for the effect you want and copy and paste it into your page.

You need to save your document on your hard disk as a 'plain text' or an 'ASCII' file (if you don't know how to do this, ask someone or check your word processor's manual). Give it a name like 'Mark's home page' and put **.html** at the end to show that it's an HTML document.

You can check how your page is looking by opening it in your browser while you're offline. Do this regularly to make sure that it's all working as you want it to.

Finding a home

Once you've created your home page you need to store your HTML and image files where other Net users can access them. To do this you need to find a host computer. Many IAPs and online services give subscribers free Web space or perhaps someone you know works for a company which will allow you to use its server for free.

You've already downloaded information from the Net but now you need to do the opposite – 'upload' your Web page to your host computer. This can be done in different ways so ask for instructions.

Tell the world about it!

Now you're the proud owner of a home page, you want everyone to visit it. You can email the address to your friends but you can't email everyone on the Internet, so register your site with the search engines. The instructions are online.

Shortcuts

Hopefully you won't find writing HTML too difficult, but if you want to take a smart shortcut to getting a Web page up on the Net, there are several sites that make it very easy for you.

These sites provide 'templates' or forms which you fill in and – hey presto! – you have a Web site. Doing it yourself from scratch is more challenging, and you have much more control over what your page looks like, but for instant results check out these spots:

EXPRESS PAGE
http://expage.com/index.html

FREEZONE HOME PAGE CONSTRUCTOR
http://www.freezone.com/hpc/

KID'S INTERACTIVE HOME PAGE MAKER
http://www.tiac.net/users/sturner/interact.html

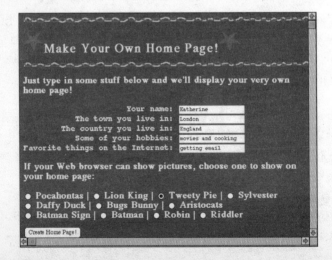

Help with home pages

Of course there is masses of information and advice on the Web about putting together your home page. Try these places:

HTML HELP FROM KIDZ
http://www.worldvillage.com/kidz/htmlhelp.htm
Lots of information and sensible advice.

CREATE YOUR OWN WEB PAGE
http://www.smplanet.com/webpage/webpage.html
More than you ever wanted to know about HTML.

WEB WORKSHOP
http://www.vividus.com/wwsample/download.html
An easy-to-use home page builder – try it free for a month.

Other Web sites

ANIMALS

- Horsefun Home Page
http://horsefun.com/index.html
Puzzles and pony tales for fans of our four-legged friends.
- Tiger Town
http://www.best.com/~hazelh/tiger.html
Find out about the efforts being made to save this endangered species.
- Watery World of Whales
http://whales.magna.com.au/index.html
Wallow in these fascinating facts and photos.

BOOKS

- Just For Kids Who Love Books
http://www.geocities.com/Athens/Olympus/1333/kids.htm
Info on authors like Roald Dahl and books like Goosebumps.
- Children's Literature Web Guide
http://www.ucalgary.ca/~dkbrown/
Loads of links about books for kids.
- Seussville
http://www.randomhouse.com/seussville/
Chat with the Cat-in-the-Hat and Sam-I-Am.

FILM

- Internet Movie Database
http://www.it.imdb.com/
Searchable information on every film ever made.
- Disney.com
http://www.disney.com/
Meet and interact with your favourite cartoon characters.
- Looney Tunes
http://www.wbanimation.com/
Ask Bugs Bunny and his friends "what's up, Doc?"

HISTORY AND GEOGRAPHY

The World of the Vikings
http://www.pastforward.co.uk/vikings/index.html
Learn about the life and times of the Norsepeople.
- National Geographic Society
http://www.nationalgeographic.com/kids/
Features great photographs and stunning virtual journeys.
- Dr Dave's UK Pages
http://www.neosoft.com/~dlgates/uk/ukpages.html
Masses of links to information about the UK.

MUSEUMS

- Internet Museum of Holography
http://www.holoworld.com/
Amazing sights and instructions for making your own hologram.
- Natural History Museum
http://www.nhm.ac.uk/
Including the dinosaur data files.
- Science Museum
http://www.nmsi.ac.uk/
Information about what's on at the real museum plus an online exhibition area.

MUSIC

- Beginners' Guide to Classical Music
http://www.rcavictor.com/rca/hits/guide/cover.html
All about the pop music of long ago.
- Pipsqueaks
http://www.childrensmusic.org/Pipsqueaks.html
A fun musical ezine.
- The Ultimate Band List
http://ubl.com/
The best list of musical links on the Web.

SCIENCE

- Exploratorium
http://www.exploratorium.edu/
Superb online science experiments.
- Explore Science
http://www.explorescience.com/
Brilliant online demonstrations of basic scientific principles.
- Star Child
http://heasarc.gsfc.nasa.gov/docs/StarChild/
An excellent introduction to the solar system.

TELEVISION

- BBC
http://www.bbc.co.uk/
The Beeb online, including Blue Peter and Children's BBC.
- The X-Files
http://www.thex-files.com/
Mysterious goings-on for Mulder and Scully fans.
- Mr Bean
http://www.mrbean.co.uk/
Oh no, it's that man again!

Other Web sites

INTERNET ACCESS PROVIDERS

In the UK, a subscription to an Internet access provider costs around £10 per month, while a subscription to an online service provider is about £5 per month for five free hours, with extra hours costing between £1 and £2.

Demon (UK)
Tel: 0181 371 1234

Easynet (UK)
Tel: 0171 681 4444

UUNet Pipex
Tel: 0500 474 739

Access One (Australia)
Tel: 1800 818 391

Ozemail (Australia)
Tel: 1800 805 874

Internet Co of NZ (New Zealand)
Tel: 09 358 1186

ONLINE SERVICE PROVIDERS

AOL (UK)
Tel: 0800 279 1234

CompuServe (UK)
Tel: 0800 289 378

MSN (UK)
Tel: 0345 002 000

FURTHER READING

There is a lot of technical advice available on the Internet itself, but the best book about the Net for grownups is *The Rough Guide to the Internet* by Angus Kennedy (published by Rough Guides).

Glossary

attachment: a document or file sent with an email
avatar: a graphic that represents a real person
bookmark: a page you save to return to
bot: a robot program used by search engines
browser: the software that allows you to access the Web
button: something you click on
case sensitive: it matters whether you use capital or small letters
chat room: an online space for talking via the keyboard
clip art: pictures you can use in your work, often for free
compression software: makes a file smaller (see decompression software)
crawler: a robot program used by search engines
decompression software: returns a file to its real size (see compression software)
default: the standard setting
demo: a demonstration or sample program
directory: a categorised list of Web sites
domain name: the name and address of a computer on the Internet
domain type: describes the host in an email address
download: transfer computer data from a Web site to your computer
email: electronic messages sent via the Internet
encryption: a way of scrambling numbers and text
Eudora: a popular email package
ezine: an electronic magazine
FAQ: frequently asked questions
favourite: a page you save to return to
frames: a way of dividing up space on a Web page
freeware: software that is free to download and use
.gif file: a type of image file common on the Web
hacker: an Internet criminal
hard copy: a paper copy of a document or image
hardware: computer equipment
hit: a relevant address generated by a search engine
home page: the first page of a Web site or the first page you see when you access the Web
host: a big computer that stores Web files or sends on email
HTML: HyperText Markup Language – the language in which Web pages are written
http: hypertext transfer protocol – the way computers send Web documents over the Internet
hyperlink: moves you to another Web page or site
IAP: short for Internet access provider – the company that connects you to the wider Internet (sometimes called ISP – Internet service provider)
Java: a computer language that adds interactivity to Web pages

Glossary

kilobits per second: a measurement of the speed at which your modem sends and receives data

kilobyte: how the size of software is measured – 1000 kilobytes equals 1 megabyte

log off: disconnect from the Internet

log on: connect to the Internet

mailbox: where email is stored

megabyte: how the size of software is measured – 1 megabyte equals 1000 kilobytes

Microsoft Internet Explorer: a popular browser

Microsoft Mail: a popular email package

modem: a box which allows your computer and the telephone system to communicate with each other

Netnanny: software that bars access to unpleasant sites

Netscape Navigator: a popular browser

Netsurf: software that bars access to unpleasant sites

offline: not connected to the Internet

online: connected to the Internet

package: another word for software

plug-in: software which provides additional features and works with your browser

search engine: a Web page which helps you search for information

secure server: a host computer which is safe to use for electronic commerce

self-extracting: a file which decompresses itself automatically

shareware: software that is free to download but a small fee must be paid to use it

signature file: appears at the bottom of email messages and describes the sender

software: the instructions that make your computer carry out different operations

specification: a description of a computer system

surfing: moving from Web page to Web page and Web site to Web site

sysop: someone who runs an online area

TCP/IP: Transmission Control Protocol/Internet Protocol – how data is moved around the Internet

template: a form to be filled in

thread: an online conversation about a particular topic which doesn't happen in real time

upgrade: to improve the speed and efficiency of software or hardware

Web site: a collection of Web pages

World Wide Web (www): a way of storing and accessing information on the Internet

Index

Index

ACTIVATORS

All you need to know

0 340 715162	Astronomy	£3.99	☐
0 340 715197	Ballet	£3.99	☐
0 340 715847	Birdwatching	£3.99	☐
0 340 715189	Cartooning (Sept 98)	£3.99	☐
0 340 715200	Computers Unlimited (Sept 98)	£3.99	☐
0 340 715111	Cycling	£3.99	☐
0 340 715219	Drawing (Sept 98)	£3.99	☐
0 340 715138	Football	£3.99	☐
0 340 715146	The Internet	£3.99	☐
0 340 715170	Riding	£3.99	☐
0 340 715235	Skateboarding	£3.99	☐
0 340 71512X	Swimming (Sept 98)	£3.99	☐

Turn the page to find out how to order these books

more info • more tips • more fun!

ORDER FORM

Books in the Activators series are available at your local bookshop, or can be ordered direct from the publisher.
A complete list of titles is given on the previous page. Just tick the titles you would like and complete the details below.
Prices and availability are subject to change without prior notice.

Please enclose a cheque or postal order made payable to Bookpoint Ltd, and send to: Hodder Children's Books, Cash Sales Dept, Bookpoint, 39 Milton Park, Abingdon, Oxon OX14 4TD.
Email address: orders@bookpoint.co.uk.

If you would prefer to pay by credit card, our call centre team would be delighted to take your order by telephone.
Our direct line is 01235 400414 (lines open 9.00 am – 6.00 pm, Monday to Saturday; 24-hour message answering service).
Alternatively you can send a fax on 01235 400454.

Title .... First name .... Surname ....

Address ....

....

....

Daytime tel .... Postcode.....................................

If you would prefer to post a credit card order, please complete the following.

Please debit my Visa/Access/Diner's Card/American Express (delete as applicable) card number:

Signature ....Expiry Date ....

If you would NOT like to receive further information on our products, please tick ☐ .